My Journey to
Spiritual Healing

My Journey to Spiritual Healing

Sunita Verma

ZORBA BOOKS

ZORBA BOOKS

Published by Zorba Books, July 2023
Website: www.zorbabooks.com
Email: info@zorbabooks.com
Author Name & Copyright © Sunita Verma
Title: My Journey to Spirituality

Paperback (ISBN):- 978-93-95217-99-6
Ebook (ISBN):- 978-93-95217-91-0

Zorba Books Pvt. Ltd. (opc)
Sushant Arcade,
Next to Courtyard Marriot,
Sushant Lok 1, Gurgaon – 122009, India

Printed in India

Table of Content

Gratitude

I dedicate my book to all my gods, divine powers, my parents, and all my teachers (Gurus). This book is a result of the blessings from all of them.

This book is the story of my journey to spirituality. I am thankful to all those who encouraged me to write this book, especially my friend, Sadhika, with whose support and guidance I could make this idea turn into reality.

How I Initiated Writing my Book

I am Sunita Verma. I was born in a middle class family, and my parents were very religious by nature.

My mother was a pious personality who imparted in us the good values of life and always showed us the right path of life. She gave all her kids higher education and never limited us from going into any field of education and/or activity. She always stood with me in every step of my life and all my achievements in any field. She was with me through my tough times and guided me. Today, she is not with us, but her valuable teachings and value for life shall always remain with us. My mother used to get up early in the morning (*Brahm Muhurat*) for her prayers and meditation. My father was a little strict, but he was also a spiritual person; after his retirement he used to sit for hours to meditate and pray. He was a devotee of Lord Shiva. Before leaving his body he told us that he was going to be a monk in his next birth.

Maybe because of my parents I have chosen this path.

I got married at the age of 24 and had a good life. After a year I was blessed with a son, and three years later God gifted me a beautiful daughter. After a few years, due to some compelling circumstances, I had to work, for which I did a course and started my own business. I gave my children good education from good institutions against my family's wishes. After schooling and completing higher education they got good jobs. Time was passing well; however, the universe wanted something else. The universe wanted my path to be different and that I should move towards the universe, so universe gave me pain. As the saying goes: "No pain, no gain," which means that nobody can achieve anything without pain or sacrifice—so if you chose the path of spirituality you have to lose something. The universe wanted my next journey to be with the universe and that I should devote my next life to human welfare (*Jankalyan*). That is why the almighty sent my children away from me, though they are very close to my heart, and in the same way, I am very close to their hearts. From there on, my journey started to serve the needful. Before this journey I decided to lead the life of an ascetic (*Sanyas*), but one of my highly spiritual friends changed my heart and advised me to write a book on spirituality. She told me that she got a message from the universe that I should write a book. **That is how I started my journey to write a book.**

How I Began my Journey to Spirituality

I had never been a spiritual person. This was my beginning toward a spiritual path. I found that the world is full of pain, grief, and suffering. I did not get Diksha from any guru, but I listened to the preaching of all gurus and tried to follow that. I started meditation and prayers. In the beginning it was a little tough as I could sit for only for 5–10 minutes for meditation, but gradually my meditating sessions could extend to hours. Sometimes I could meditate with much ease, and at times I could not as my mind used to divert to different places. I used to listen to Sri Ravi Shankar Ji who always says that just as you brush your teeth daily, in the same way, you should sit for meditation as a morning ritual. Occasionally I could reach deep in meditation and sometimes not. I was getting detached from this world but I had to reach toward spirituality while living in the world (Family Life). I started praying for more than 10 hours a day. Since my childhood I used to pray to Devi Maa. Now that I prayed more and with such sincerity, one day Devi Maa became happy and I could see the divine form of Durga Maa. I was really blessed after seeing her. But my journey did not stop there. I had to get more than that, and I wanted to reach the universe. It seems to be the blessings of my karmas, which changed my whole life and this day came in my life (Darshan of Maa). I started spending maximum time in *puja paath* (Prayers). I thought either of God or the universe, but I did not stop there. I started chanting Lord Shivji's mantras day and night and used to sleep for maximum four hours a day. Then, one day, even Bhole baba became happy and blessed me with his darshan (Vision).

For me, this was a very new experience (I am an unwise, ignorant, unintelligent, and innocent). Although I am a very simple person, I got these blessings. For that I am thankful to God. God has given us this life; we are blessed with this invaluable treasure. We should nurture spirituality in this life. God has given us five senses (touch, smell, taste, sight, and sound). If we win over our five senses, our sixth sense will develop, that is, intuition. It is not easy to win over intuition. But if we do win over it, then more issues like detachment and/or sometimes not being happy with ourselves arise and we keep on fighting with them; if we will win over it them our six sense will rise, and that is meeting with almighty, and thus we connect with the universe. This is when we leave our ego and pride and connect with the real energy. I am writing this with my spiritual friend Swati, who is a Reiki healer. She told me about Reike, its holy strength, and its benefits. She recommended that I should learn reiki.

The World of Reiki Healing, its Experience, and its Benefits

Reiki is a positive energy from the universe. Discovered by Dr. Mikao usui in 1922 AD, this is a Japanese technique which is also a part of Yoga.

Some people believe that Reiki originated in India. Thousands of years ago, saints (Rishi Munis) used to perform touch-healing to cure people. It is a Japanese word which means energy from the universe. It is a technique that enables healers to receive energy from the universe, transform it into a desirable form, and transfer it toward a needful subject/ person. The meaning of Reiki is universal energy; it is more than a science—Healing powers of Reiki alone have worked where doctors have suggested operation (I have proof for this statement).

Reiki is a treasure of universe's energy and knowledge which can solve many problems like ailment, depression, stress, etc. Its energy can give happiness.

Benefits of Reiki

Reiki's benefits include relationship healing, addiction healing, disease healing, achieving goals, and more.

First, I learned two levels of Reiki, following which I decided to move forward, completed my 3rd level, and started giving healing to others with the energy of the universe. The results I found in Reiki is power such that no other treatment contains, so I decided to move forward and learned Level 4A from my Guruji (AVM). With his blessing I received my

Grand Master degree and continued practicing healing. I dedicated 24 hours of the day to those who needed healing, and when they were cured I would feel such inner happiness that I couldn't get from any other source.

reiki is a technique that enables healers to receive universal energy and transfer the same toward healing people and resolving their problems. It is a natural healing ability through the power of the ancient. Reiki is the universal life enforcement healing energy (it means *universe ki energy*). I also learned Reiki symbols from my Guruji (AVM) and then got attuned to practice. We also do different types of meditation. Since Reiki is a positive energy it never harms anyone in any way. The experience of learning Reiki and practicing and receiving power of the universe changed my life completely.

Learning Reiki and Lama Fera and Their Experience

After Reiki I learned "Lama Fera" from Sir Sanjay Gupta's book and his knowledge. This technique was founded under Buddhism and was spread in the world by Buddhist monks. This is a very powerful technique. Lama means Sadguru (Saint), and Fera means powerful positive universal energy. As energy this can even heal plants and animals. I feel blessed that I got this opportunity to learn this technique, and with this I feel more energized. As a part of this healing technique we get energy from Lord Buddha's powerful energy, and we gain our spiritual power as well. With Lama Fera's technique people are cured promptly. Sound healing is also a part of this technique; this opens all the chakras swiftly and removes negative energies.

My Experiences of Reiki and Lama Fera and Feedback

Seven year old girl who could not speak or listen — With the extraordinary powers of the universe and healing, within one month she started to speak the word "OM," and within the next 6 months she started listening and speaking.

Feedback of parents — Thank you very much, ma'am for blessing my baby as a Reiki healer. My 7-year-old daughter had speech and hearing impairment, and now she has started listening and speaking very well through Reiki healing within a span of only six months. Thank you so much, ma'am

– Chandrasekhar Karole, Sachive Colony, near Dreamland City, Multai, District Betul, UP

Thank you aunty for helping my husband. He got a job in merely five days of healing. May god bless you with all the happiness and abundance. You keep helping all of us with the help of healing and your prayers

– Nidhi, Gurgaon

Thanks, didi, I am blessed to have you in my life at this stage. Well, as you know I have been trying to sell my property in Noida since a long time, and every time at the last minute of the final deal something would happen and the deal wouldn't conclude. With your prayers and support, when I contacted suddenly my property was sold and I am very thankful to you

– Ankur Malhotra, Gurgaon

I want to thank you and Maa for the blessings and support during my tough time. Under your Reiki consultation I am feeling alive. You have upheld and lifted my morale and provided relief to me from my problems by your spiritual practice. God really has a direct connection with your truthful soul and have positive vibes that I feel during the consultation. I myself feel and accept that due to prayers I overcame, and the lower part of my body recovered. Now I can confidently perform my daily activities and have got my confidence back. I hope and pray your mentorship and blessings will continue. Thanks, Didi.

– Mayank, Dwarka Delhi

Sunita is a great Reiki healer. Despite being so knowledgeable she is very meek and humble. Her biggest strength is her selfless service. My Reike experience with Sunita has been amazing. She is an expert in distant Reiki — My daughter was going through a complicated pregnancy where baby in the womb was not gaining weight. Doctors had told us to be prepared for a premature delivery any time. It was only due to her constant healing-focused prayers and positive energy that we were able to overcome all the medical challenges. I am grateful to God and her that I have been blessed with a completely healthy granddaughter. Throughout our difficult times she was ready to receive phone calls at any hour of the day and would take regular feedback from me regarding the doctor's visit and baby's growth. Her Reiki sessions are very powerful and show instant results. She is a bundle of professionalism, love, and care. Thank you, Sunita, for coming in my life like a guardian, mentor, and healer

– Mrs. Verma, Canada

Thank you, aunty, for healing my daughter in the middle of the night, going the extra mile waking up on one call and providing her healing when she had a temperature of 103 on a chilled winter night. We were so worried. Thank you, aunty, for healing her with your superpowers. Jai Mata Di

– Nidhi, Gurgaon

I had gone to Jim Corbett Park to attend a family wedding and suddenly my brother's health deteriorated. He had a temperature of 104, and we didn't know what to do as there was no doctor available in the vicinity that we could consult. That is when I got in touch with Sunita ji and told her about my brother's condition. She, along with a co-healer, immediately started the healing and within a span of 15–20 minutes his temperature was normal, and slowly he recovered further and was in good condition to attend the rest of the wedding. Thank you Sunita ji and the Universe

– Lata, Gurgaon

All the above experiences of divine power have changed my life completely.

Third Eye Opening

Then I did third eye opening from my Guruji at AVM. The third eye is a spiritual eye located just above the physical eyes. It is said to be the site where we receive physical impressions, although there are instances in which the third eye opens suddenly. It is usually a gradual process. There are several exercises that you can use to open your third eye.

1. We release any blockages that we may have.
2. We visualize our chakras.
3. Meditation helps to focus and relax the mind.

We have to practice opening our third eye. We can see the hidden world after our third eye opens; we can read others' mind; there is no confusion in our mind, and our intuition never fails. We gain control over our mind. In Hinduism, we call it an *ajana chakra,* and in Buddhism we call it the eye of consciousness. The third eye chakra is closely associated with life. Our energy rises, and we see more colors and become more conscious. After our third eye opens we have more dreams and get hidden messages from the universe, and our spiritual will becomes deeper. But without guru's guidance we should not try to open our third eye as this can be harmful for us. If we do this without a guide we can end up in harmful energy and other problems.

Angel Therapy and Astral Travel

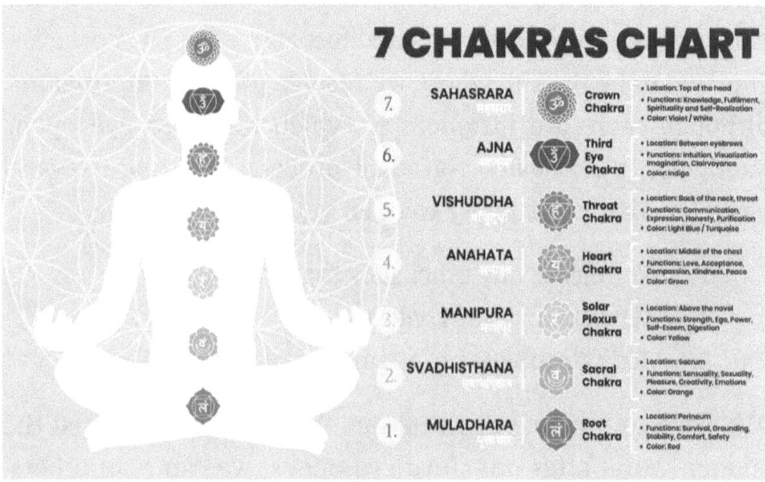

Then I learned the Angel healing course, which are symbols of love and light. Angel derives from the Greek word "angelos," a translation of a Hebrew word meaning **"messenger."** They were mentioned in recorded history as far back as 3000 B.C. and were present in ancient cultures of Egypt, Babylon, Persia, and India. Perhaps, they were not called "angels." Angel in the ancient cultures is acknowledged of being winged in higher consciousness. Some Native American teachings also include angels.

They don't have a physical body and are messengers from the heaven here to help us. Angel connection course teaches us to establish connection with angels. They are at a higher level than us, so they can see things more clearly than humans can. They have strong magnetic strength and help us feel like a spiritual human being, connected to the universe. We are God's loving children, and we can also get spiritual powers if we wish.

Angel Therapy and Astral Travel

Angel Therapy

We all have two guardian angels that are always with us. They also have specialities and interests that are suited to guide you in your path and purpose. Angels work with us through sending us spiritual and healing energies. When we feel pulsations or vibrations through our body, that can be energies from angels, but we can only feel this when we are connected to angels. Angelic guidance is always loving, uplifting, and inspiring.

Angels are completely dedicated to helping humanity spiritually as well as in practical ways. My experiences with angels are synonymous to the above belief and concepts.

Astral Travel

I did the Astral Travel course from AVM. It is a different level, where while some people do not believe in this travel world, others have experienced the journey. As a part of this travel, one goes out of body and then comes back — Astral body is a form of consciousness similar to our physical body.

After deep meditation we get more energy from the universe, and we discover our soul plan through astral travel. When we receive sufficient amount of energy we can perceive astral body traveling beyond space and time. During meditation, after receiving abundant cosmic energy, consciousness in our body starts moving. We feel jerks in our whole body, and our body feels like it is floating. We feel lightness of our body like a feature. After this energy the movement of our astral body starts coming out of the physical body with a link called **silver cord.** Silver cord is nothing but a high consciousness which transfers from physical body to astral body and vice versa. This helps us to do astral travel. While doing astral travel we get higher knowledge of self.

In astral travel, our astral body can pass through all physical materials and elements like earth, water, wind, and fire. Astral body can go to any other frequency without any limitation. With this we come to know that we are not just mind and body; but if we stay in our body, our limit will vanish. We understand that we are limitless. We also understand that we are consciousness; we understand the new dimension of life. We came to know with these experiences that we never die; it's only our body which goes and our soul always travels. We are infinity; we get unique experiences during astral travel journey.

Past Life Regression Therapy

After completing astral travel I felt that the universe has unlimited things for us to learn. I approached AVM (Vikas sir), and he suggested me to do Past Life Regression Therapy, so I started this course. In this course, we learned that the problems we face in this birth are somehow related to our previous birth. We have to undergo our last life's errors and misdeeds in this birth. These are our karmas that we have to face in this birth. With this course, our foresight is heightened. If we are scared of anything like water, sea, or height after reaching in the last birth, we come to know the reason of the problem we face in this birth. For going (reaching) in last birth we have to do meditate intensely, so that our mind is fresh and free from all the unnecessary thoughts stored in our brain, so that we can easily reach the last birth.

My experience: After meditating for about an hour I reached in my last birth. I saw my mother was the same as in this birth, and she was young. I had two small children. My husband always used to fight with me, and one day, he came to beat me. I ran and jumped in a well, and I saw Durga Maa lifting my soul upward to the universe. Now I know why Durga Maa is always with me in this lifetime, and I can always feel her presence. I could not complete my karmas in the last birth, so I had to complete my karmas in this birth. Before doing this course, I repeatedly thought of committing suicide, but after seeing my last birth I never thought it again, and this thought is out of my mind now. My purpose of telling this is that we should never think of ending life, as after suicide either our soul wanders or we have to complete our karmas in the next birth. We are blessed with this beautiful life; we should live it with the wishes and blessings of the universe. We should bear our pain and pleasures (Ups and Downs of life). With prayers and sadhna our pain diminishes. Angels and the universal positive energies come to guide and help us, and our pains are alleviated.

Changes That I Noticed in My Life

After reaching the past life I felt that my ego which I had before vanished, but I had to increase meditating duration. I used to get up at God's hour, the time of the creator (Brahma Muhurat), which was a divine gift for me. Early in the morning I feel that divine powers have come to wake me up, and subsequently when I would sit for meditation I felt new experiences.

Now I enjoy every blessing of nature like trees, birds, river, and hills; I can sit and behold these natural beauties for hours, and I feel them inside me. With meditation I was connected with the powers within me, and the purpose of my life was changed. My behavior toward others changed, and there were no complaints and grumbling. Now, within me there was forgiveness for other people and myself. I had to work on my conscience (Soul) as my soul was still not pure; there were too many thoughts in my mind. I had to come out of it so that I could be free from unnecessary worries as they destroy our mental as well as spiritual energies. For example, if we look at any beauty of nature we see its splendor, but if our brain is confused then we won't be able to appreciate this splendor. If we are at peace we can think and understand more. Now, the motto of my life was creating a happy life.

The right motto can help create a life filled with joy and purpose instead of one that leaves you feeling lost and directionless. It can be with spiritual journey or serving people in any way. Now I feel that my life before this spiritual journey was aimless. Spiritual journey has had a metamorphosis effect (*kaya palat*) on my life. Spiritual journey is awakening of higher life. Before this awakening I used to get upset of trivial things or small problems. And then I found the power of sun and experienced its energy. Sunbath is beneficial for mind and body. Sunlight is the food for our cells. With the daily sunbath I found extraordinary energy and power in me. Direct sunbath is beneficial for us as this removes our negative energy and sharpens our memories. It raises our sixth sense too. Sunlight is helpful for both heart and body. Sunbath cleans our inner body. We should express gratitude to the sun and thank it for giving us extraordinary energy. We can do *sun tratak kriya* (six yogic cleaning technique); it improves our eyesight and raises our intuitive power; however, we should do it only when the sun rises. We attain siddhis from *Sun Tratak Kriya* and receive higher level of energy of the universe with this kriya. It has changed me a lot. I am more sympathetic with people, no matter if I know them or not, and now I believe more in the energy of the universe and people with good souls.

Obstruction in the Course of Spiritual Journey

After this blessed episode, again some negative energy in the form of human being tried to push me back from my cosmic journey. I felt mentally harassed, and this was an attempt to distract me from my meditation. But their efforts failed as I was so determined toward my spiritual journey that I was able to defeat every negative energy that came in my path. The more that energy tried to push me back, the more I felt determined to fight it and stay on my path. I had to win against every negative energy, and I won. I want to say that if I can go ahead on my spiritual journey despite of all these negative energies, then anyone and everyone can.

This spirituality is one path which keeps us away from Lust (Kaam), wrath (Krodh), greed (Lobh), attachment (Moh), and ego. This is the path of peace not only for us but also for the whole world. Every person is wandering in search of peace, and if they find the path of spirituality they will get peace, and their souls will be satisfied (I speak from my own experiences).

Adhyatam, Dhyan, and Sadhna

I did a course "Art of Living" by Sri Sri Ravi Shankar. During this course I learned how to make life better, richer, and balanced whether it is happiness or sorrow. We should accept every individual as they are and should be happy in any circumstances. We should always forgive others, and we should live in the present. I also learned *sudharshan kriya* and *pranayama* and found it very beneficial for me; I felt improvement in my health. With breathing exercises, not only our body but also our mind is revived, and our soul feels pure. After breathing exercises, we have control on our emotions. We are happy all the time and feel positive thoughts eliminating all negative ones.

Then I experienced one more miracle in my spiritual journey while meditating. I used to see a Yogi Mahatma. I saw him for many days during meditation. I used to see (vision) him in an ashram near a temple in Haridwar. So one day I felt that this was a message from the universe, and I must go there to find that Yogi Ji. While I was planning to go there, someone told me that with God's blessing a mahatmaji has arrived here for Gita Pravachan who is 110 years old. I went there to seek his blessings, and as I reached there I saw the same Mahatmaji that I used to see during meditation. I was totally numb and couldn't speak a word, but after some time I was inarticulate with joy. What else did I want from my faith in the universe? I felt so blessed that I can't explain.

People are running harum-scarum for material gains. If they reach inside them, they will find cosmic energies, and after finding these energies many of their problems will be solved. If the lady of the house is spiritual, the whole family will be spiritual and with good souls. Even though I am not so knowledgeable, I am saying all of this based on my personal experiences. We should remove negative thoughts from our mind and be always positive. By remaining positive, our body and mind will work fantastically. Our mind and body are the most valuable gifts given to us by the universe, so we should respect and love them.

We can give instructions to our body as we want, only that there should be firm determination in what we want or have to do in order to meet God. When we are disappointed, the universe and positive energies hold our hand. Blessings of the universe are always with us. If we call Him from our conscience (Antaratma), the divine energies bless us so much that we cannot even imagine. The Sadhak who gets the love and blessings from the Almighty doesn't need anything else in this world. But when we experience all these, we should tell others all about this so that they can also experience the same. We should spread the knowledge we get about the Almighty, and we will get more blessings and knowledge. If we want to meet divine powers we have to do more sadhana to reach there. The people who believe in God are always devoted to those energies. God gives us pleasure and pain, ups and downs in life; we should accept both. When we are deeply connected to God, he will surely show his presence but we might not feel that. When we are deeply connected with God, the Almighty will not leave us, but to reach there we need *tapasya* or *tap*. The more we pray, the closer we will be to God. If we want to reach divine power, we will have to leave materialistic world activities. God is within us; we just have to receive the energies. Divine powers are always happy with our unconditional services (seva), like cow-seva. If we want to be with divine powers, we will surely get it, only that we have to get up in the Brahm mahurat and meditate. After some time with these efforts of ours, we will be Sadhak or Sadhika. As per my own experience with this positive attitude as God's power, experiences in meditation, and company of saints (Rishi-Muni), we can reach high spirituality; we can be more at peace and not care about the problems.

If we go near the universe (in meditation or sadhana), the universe will definitely hold us and we will get answers to all our problems. The universe gives us messages in different ways, sometimes in dreams, sometimes with other indications.

Our mind is full of negativity. We have to clean our mind first for any meditation. When we are without any stress, we get more energy and then we can sit in meditation. This way we have our soul and we get peace. We will be able to think more, and we will be happy not only from outside but also from within our inner soul.

Spirituality and meditation—the aim of my life is to be happy and at peace. It can be from spiritual journey or to serve people. I realized that my life was useless and there was no meaning before this spiritual journey. My journey changed me completely. Before this, I always felt that life is full of problems and complications, but now nothing affects me.

To reach my inner soul and to know myself I kept *maun vrat*. With this I could know myself—who I am and what I want. After maun vrat I could feel the universe more deeply. The deeper we go in maun and meditation, the more we get to know about the universe.

Maun should not be just about being silent with words, but also we should be quiet from the inside. But we must not trouble or torture ourselves with this. In maun, our soul should stand still like a pond. We get peace and happiness and solution of our every problem. We get new ideas, and negative thoughts are expelled from within us. With maun we reach inside us and we get more energy. We come to know ourselves. With spirituality, we reach deeper, and our capacity for tolerance increases.

My experience in maun was that I reached my inner soul and got enlightened with the white light inside me. I feel closer to divine energies.

But still there were negative energies which distracted me from my journey. Gradually, I started to detach myself from loved ones, was going on my path with Dhyan sadhana, was getting rid of my negative energies, and my ego was vanished. The purpose of writing all this is that all of us can go onto this path. This path takes us away from lust, anger, greed, attachment, and jealousy.

Anger takes us away from our spiritual path. With anger, our hormones are imbalanced; mental stress, blood pressure, and heart ailments grow. So, we should stay away from anger. If we sit for sadhana for hours and then get angry for 5 minutes, all our energies will get converted into negative ones. Our motto in life is to get rid of negativity. We should live happily. If the whole world decides not to get angry, it will be at peace. Then comes attachment—too much attachment hurts. We should be attached with others up to some limit. If we are too much attached with anybody, we won't be able to go on our journey. Lord Krishna says that attachment lessens our intelligence. When we are too much attached, we will be involved in materialistic gains rather than spirituality. When we are extremely attached, we won't be able to know the difference between right and wrong.

Attachment causes pain; as when we love our children too much and they grow up and leave us, we won't be able to tolerate. So, attachment should be up to some limit. It is better to be attached with God. The more we will go near God, the more power, energy, and love of the universe we will get. So, we should be less attached with materialistic things and more engaged in Dhyaan and spirituality.

Our biggest strength is the spiritual strength within, so we should always thank the universe for giving us the mind, body, and soul during the spiritual journey. When we get up in the morning we should thank God for a new day. Ever noticed that even animals look upward to the universe as they are thanking God for the food they are getting? Most of the players also look upward after every success. Then why do we always forget to thank the universe for our achievement. If we thank the universe for every small thing, our negativity will change into positivity. We should be thankful for God's each creation like trees, plants, flowers, sun, moon, sky, and stars, followed by being thankful to our parents who have given us this beautiful human body and brought us up with good values. We should be thankful to our teachers (Gurus) who have taught us a lot, as a result of which we are here. And finally, we should be thankful to the universe that has given us this lovely family.

This cosmic energy of the universe is everywhere, but we are unable to receive it as we don't want to see what the universe and gurus showed us — the path of self-realization and internal self-purification. We should not be slaves of our conscious mind and should think of self-purification; only then we can derive delight and give others the pleasure of life.

But on the path of spirituality, it is not easy to reach our destination. We have to face lot of hurdles. I also had to go through them in every step of my journey. Negative energies stop us in our path of spirituality, but we should not stop there and should continue our journey.

After these experiences I tried to reach within. This was the beginning of my journey (The practice of going inside without worries and focusing on my breath going in and coming out). Breathing it in (breath) will touch all the live aspects of ours, and breathing out will expel the negative thoughts. This is the natural process when our intellect is not working. Meditation has a deep connection with the breath. When we observe our breath continuously, we are away from the rest of the surroundings. Our breath works differently depending on our moods; for example, when we are angry our breath is very fast, but when we are calm our breath will be normal. When we go in deep meditation while observing our breath, we have different types of experiences; our cosmic energy improves, and we can control our breath because if we can't control our breath then how could we control ourselves and the problems of life? We should control our frame of mind so that we can go in deep meditation.

We are blessed that we belong to such a great country in which sages (Rishi-Muni) with their Jap-Tup (Prayers and meditation) invented stars and planets long back which our scientists are discovering now or only some time back. We can also discover cosmic energy, and with meditation we can get energies from the universe which is the same for everyone, and there is no religion or caste in the universe. Its energy is the same for everyone. After connecting with the universe, we get a lot of pleasure which we don't get in this materialistic world. Happiness in this materialistic world is temporary.

As we take energy from the universe we reach deep within us, and our inner darkness converts into bright light.

In meditation, every cell of our inner body awakens, and our thinking and desire change into the purity of soul. With deep meditation, the meditator (Sadhak) feels a fall of ambrosia from the universe.

Now I am going to talk about another experience on the night of full moon (Purnima)

The importance of Purnima night meditation is different as it increases positive energy, considering the moon is closer to the earth on that day. Some say that on such a night people with depression feel more depressed and people with higher energy get more energy.

Every Purnima night I sit for meditation (sharing one of my full moon experiences). I was in deep meditation, and I felt that the *crown chakra* was cracking. I could not understand what was happening. The next morning when I was in deep meditation I felt a bright light in my crown chakra. Then I understood that there were divine powers in my crown chakra. After this experience I was thrilled.

If you want to attain God, we have to open our minds and heart as God is all pervading. God is not in our body but in our soul. God is inside, and like we should open doors and windows of our house to let rays of the sun come in, with same way we should open our hearts and mind to attain God. For achieving this, we have to give time to ourselves as we cannot attain God in one day. God is there inside us; when we meet our soul we meet God. We should have faith in God as He will protect us from negativity. He is the creator of plants and trees which give us oxygen, which is air purifier. He is also taking care of all creatures like birds and animals equally. We should love, devote, and surrender before God and do sadhna (meditation) to attain God.

To meet the universe and go we have to meditate, and to reach deep in meditation we have to leave our thoughts. It is not necessary to sit for hours and close your eyes to meditate. While we are watching the sun, moon, or flowers for long, quietly, that is also meditation. For meditation we don't need to run from here to there; we can simply sit in peace and meditate. In the 24 hours, even if we sit for half an hour to meditate, we completely dedicate ourselves and resolve to be fully dedicated to infinite highness (means we have to dissolve I, the self — *main*).

While we are in meditation, sometimes our hands and feet feel numb; sometimes we feel something is happening in our head; sometimes there is heaviness in our body; occasionally we feel more energy in ourselves; sometimes even our third eye opens, and sometimes we travel into the clouds while meditating. In *brahm muhurat,* if we sit for hours in meditation with our eyes closed and we suddenly open eyes and look at the sky, we can see hidden stars which scientists can see only with telescope. With deep meditation, we can overpower our feelings; we can be in control, and mind doesn't divert (wander) from here to there.

During meditation we should go deep and forget about anything else. We should be normal in all circumstances then only we will be capable of solving all the problems either from home or workplace. With meditation, our sixth sense becomes active, and we are more intellectual. Any negativity of a negative person doesn't affect us. Instead of criticizing negative people, spiritual people try to make them positive.

We don't get angry or distracted easily. If any sadhak loves or adores anyone, they should uplift that person. If one cannot do so, they should try and remove negativity.

For attaining God we have to do a lot of sadhna because without meditation or sadhna we cannot reach or see the vision of God. We have to purify our soul and be a complete devotee of God. We have to give time to reach there. We should control our minds, stay positive, and remove all negativities from our mind. We should also keep our mind away from worldly things, as once we achieve divine consciousness, we will gain spiritual prospective. We cannot be expert in one day to be spiritual and sadhak. If we plant a sapling we need to protect it; we have to take care of it. We are careful of the sapling for water and sunlight, and once it becomes a huge tree there is no need to worry. Nobody can harm it. In the same way, if we start sadhna we have to be careful with the plant of sadhna in our heart. Once we achieve the result, no negativity can harm us.

To go in deep meditation is empowerment. We should keep our mind and body in control. We should remember good memories of the past; we should keep away negative memories from us as they lower our energies in meditation. Bad memories distract us from our path of *dhayana,* but sometimes for negative circumstances or people we go deep in meditation to avoid those negative circumstances. There are times we are extremely disturbed. However, because of negative people we find the way of spirituality. As I have mentioned before, I am thankful to those negative situations and people; to keep myself away from them I decided to do meditation and lot of prayers and Jap-Tap. We should not give up in any situation; we should find another way to reach the universe.

If we want to be with God, we have to be polite and humble. When we are humble, we get more energy and more spiritual knowledge. But if there is ego and pride in us, our cosmic energy will be less or will vanish. If we want to attain the Almighty, we don't have to bring ego or pride with us. For a true sadhak, all people are the same; it doesn't matter if they are rich or poor or belong to any caste. When we get success in something, some people forget that every human being is the same. If we forget that, our downfall in spirituality begins, and the energy and knowledge we have earned in years will vanish. If we are full of ego and pride people will start staying away from us, so we should be very polite and humble to be able to reach somewhere. If anybody behaves badly with us, we should not get annoyed; rather, we should tolerate that and should pray to God to give that person good sense (Sadbudhi). If we hear criticism, we should think deeply and logically where we went wrong (Chintan-Manan), and we should accept criticism — this should be our path. If anybody appreciates us, we should take it sportingly. In meditation, we should be kind with everyone. Only if we are kind and think about others before ourselves and sacrifice, only then we will be on the right path of meditation.

For sadhna, we should work on ourselves first, only then we will be able to feel the pain of others; only then we can be successful in sadhna or meditation.

We should be thankful also for those who have shown us the path of spirituality and meditation. Sometimes negative people meet us and we are badly hurt by them and go toward the path of prayers. We should be thankful to them also, as I have mentioned earlier.

This morning I gained one more experience in my meditation. I felt fire in myself, which was one more gift to me from the universe, and I was so blessed with this. Before this, I was mentally disturbed; perhaps universe was giving me punishment for any of my mistakes. But when we are near to the universe and we are disappointed and disturbed, the universe takes us in its lap and blesses us with its new experiences.

A sadhak should be balanced and in state of peace in any circumstances. If we are balanced, cosmic energies are with us. When we are in pride or ego, the universe punishes us, and we get less universal energies. Sadhak should not be emotional. If we want to know the universe, one birth is not enough, and it is very difficult to know the universe fully. With the duties and responsibilities of the household life we might falter on every step, and during the spiritual path we might get shaken multiple times.

The person who doesn't leave the path of spirituality is the real sadhak and is also able to manage the duties of household. Generally, people do sadhna during a later part of the life; however, that is late. At that time we can do sadhna while living with family, and this is not difficult.

Few people can move to the spiritual path; one can go to the spiritual path as deep as they want. The universe indicates to us in many ways — like if we get up in Braham muhurat, it is when divine powers are around us. Spiritual people never think bad of others or say negative things for others and have the spirit of sympathy for others. They are always positive and prefer to be surrounded by positive people. They like to read good books and want to be a pure soul. Spiritual people leave their past behind, which helps them become successful in their journey. We reach inside us to win ourselves and stay positive, as Yogis are never negative. Weak people can't reach spirituality. Spiritual people are never angry; they also are always calm. There are many hindrances in the path of sadhna. If we get scared of these obstacles, we won't be able to do sadhna. The people who are devoted in dhyan can become complete yogis in sadhna. They can see the future easily and are always connected to God. True yogis have divine power. In sadhna and meditation we come to know ourselves better. As a sadhak we need to energize ourselves to reach our soul; we should keep our soul and mind pure. Our thinking should also be pure. Self-realization and consciousness of God Almighty are present in sadhna. We should be relaxed and happy during sadhna. If we are happy, the Almighty will make us happier. It is like when we throw a ball in the universe, the same ball will return back to us. So, if we are happy, more happiness will come to us, and if we are always sad or negative, more sadness will come (this is the law of nature). If we want to live in peace we should expand ourselves in enlightenment and should not become weak in any circumstance.

In meditation we see colors and light when we go deep in dhayan. Also, when we get energy in our different chakras, we see different colors. When energy is in *mooldhar chakra*, it is red; in *sacrek chakra* it is orange; in *Manipur chakra* it is yellow; in heart it is green; throat is sky blue; third eye is light purple, and in crown it is purple. In the same way we see light during meditation. But this is not achieved in one day; for this we have to do sadhna for a long time.

Apart from this, we can see five elements (earth, water, fire, air, sky) in meditation, like the color of air is transparent or white; color of fire is red; color of water is blue or light blue; color of earth is yellow, and sky is golden yellow. However, we can see these colors only in deep meditation.

Fear in spirituality - Fear is the Source of Negativity

If we are in fear of anything in spirituality, it keeps us away from our path. In sadhna, fear means that we are again with ourselves instead of being with the universe. When we are in sadhna, the fear should not be there. If there is any kind of fear, we will come down from the higher level, which means we are not able to control our thoughts and we are still living in materialistic world. There is no match between materialism and sadhna — so, what I mean is that we should be away from any kind of fear such as "what will happen to me?" or any type of negative thoughts. We have to be in peace, and we should control our emotions. Fear is a natural feeling which should not come in the way of spirituality. The universe takes our test, as we are in extreme fear we think of our spirituality. We should always be devoted to god.

When we are in sadhna with our household life, it is not difficult to do sadhna. This is a challenge to us. Fear comes in our actual test by the universe. We should not live in imaginations like this or that bad things may happen. We should be normal in any circumstance and control our emotions, only then we will be able to connect with the universe. We should be emotionally strong enough to keep away fear or any type of negativity from us, so that we get more energy, positivity, and knowledge.

In meditation we should let go attachment. We should be attached to anybody up to only some limit, as limitless attachment take us back from our path of meditation. Extreme attachment leads us to suffering. When we detach from people, we attach to God. If we are attached with human beings, we will be joyful and happy. But that happiness is temporary. If we are attached with God, we will get permanent happiness. And only then we will come to know that we are spiritual people. When we are attached with God, we will be detached from our self and this materialistic world. Being detached from others and attached with the supreme powers is the virtue of knowledge. We come to know what is right and what is wrong. And then we don't have attraction toward any materialistic thing. Our love should be unconditional love. We should not love our children so much and burden them with our love. Our love toward our children should only be in limit, so that they should not think that their parents are weak. Because if our children leave us or go somewhere else, we will not be hurt badly or suffer too much pain. We should be attached with anyone only up to a limit. But we can love limitlessly so that we will be near to God and be more attached with the Almighty, and he will not leave us. We should be attached with dhyan, sadhna, and spirituality, so that we have a stronger bond with the divine.

Power of Subconscious Mind (Maan)

Our subconscious mind is our best friend. We can mold it as much as we like. It has got a conscious aspect, which we know, and the other is subconscious, which we are not aware of. It depends upon our emotional attitude and fear—all these are in our subconscious mind. When our five senses are awakened, our spiritual journey starts, and our subconscious mind has pure thoughts. We should not think about past or future; we should only think about the present to be able to achieve spirituality in us. Only if we win over our subconscious mind will we be able to get spiritual powers. If our subconscious mind is weak, our determination to reach the universe will be shattered. So we should be strong enough so that no negative thoughts should invade our mind. If we want to sit for meditation, we have to control our subconscious mind first. If our subconscious mind is not in our control, we won't be able to reach our goal (the universe). Our main intention is sadhna. If our subconscious mind dominates us, we won't be able to become sadhak.

Sadhak's main power is to have control on them. A sadhak should not be weak. We should be strong enough to face any circumstance and don't let our self be emotionally weak. We should always be positive and not negative because when we have negative thoughts our subconscious mind will be programmed accordingly, and we would be programming our mind without realizing the results. Sometimes we program our mind positively and sometimes negatively; if we think negatively the universe will make things negative, that is why we should always be positive to bring happiness in our life (my own experience).

Pride or Arrogance

We should never be arrogant or proud. Pride causes downfall of sadhna and destroys our power of spirituality. When there is ego of spirituality, knowledge of anyone will be down. If we are proud of money, it is futile; it never stays put; it moves from one place to another.

There is difference between pride and proud – like if our children top their class, we are proud of them. But if we say we have stores of gyan or spirituality, it is our pride of arrogance. An arrogant person always wants importance or respect for oneself. A humble person always gives respect to others. Pride comes before fall. In pride as we think ourselves above others our path of spirituality will be away from us.

If we get rid of our ego we will find ourselves on the path of spirituality. if we find ourselves wrong at any point, we should admit it and feel ashamed of our self. If we are always arrogant, people around us will shy away from us. So we should never think of ourselves as a superior human being. If we are polite with everyone and bow before them, our ego will vanish. If every moment we are away from pride we will reach sadhna promptly. In pride we think we are great spiritual persons, but if we look at the universe we come to know that we are not so; we are not even a portion/part of it. We should not be egoistic but self-confident, only then we will be able to do dhayan. Self-awakening is also important. After every achievement in spirituality, our confidence increases. I am again re-iterating that we should not be proud or arrogant, only then we will be on the real path of spirituality. Our body will be destroyed one day, then why be egoistic?

Jealousy (Envy)

A spiritual person should never be jealous of anyone because he will never be happy. This way, he thinks that the other person is superior to me, and this thing cannot let him live happily. If we are not happy, how can we do sadhna or meditation? So instead of being jealous of others, we should focus on the love of God. In sadhna, one should feel others' suffering and help them get out of it, while if someone is happy we should be happy for them as there is no place for jealously or envy in the life of a sadhak. A sadhak should be normal in any circumstance, whether it is happiness or sorrow. Instead of being jealous of others, we should think of their progress to help them reach the path of spirituality. Thus, the universe will be happy with us, and we will be able to reach our goals?

Food

Food is very important in life of a sadhak because we get energy from it. A sadhak only eats vegetarian food. If we look at animals, non-vegetarian animals are lions, and vegetarian are peaceful like cows. We should eat food for the need of energy and need of our body. A sadhak should eat raw vegetables (which one can digest) and fruits. Sadhak should eat light fruits and should finish the last meal by 7 pm, which should be very light as food affects our mental health. By eating pure food one becomes more spiritual. We should pray and thank God for the food we get as they have a lot of effect. For example, if we eat Prasad in mandir or gurudwara the food tastes better than normal or home food because Prasad includes chanting/ prayers as a part of them, so we should be grateful to God for the food that we get.

Forgiveness

Now we will talk about forgiveness. When we forgive others, we reform our karmic account. When we are angry with someone and we want to take revenge, that will only be not good for our self. So when we forgive someone, it is for our own peace, and we forgive our self also. If we don't forgive others and hate them, it is like a poison that we are giving to our soul. So when we forgive others, we feel peace in our self. Our relationship will also improve if we forgive that person. If we stay angry with others, we reduce our energy, and we won't be able to do sadhna after that. Also, we will be in a negative zone, and this will affect our thoughtfulness, and we will be disturbed and restless. We should also ask for forgiveness from the universe for the mistakes we have done knowingly or unknowingly, and we will be emotionally healthy after seeking forgiveness. If we have all other qualities but forgiveness, we will not be able to become sadhak, as a sadhak who forgives anyone is a real sadhak. They are divine, and divine powers accept them. That is why they go deep in sadhna. Remember if we are on the path of sadhna and we have forgiveness, our children will also follow the same path.

Yoga

With Reiki, prayers, and sadhna, I also give importance to yoga in my life. Yoga is very necessary in life as it is a gift given to us by our saints (Rishi-Muni) ages ago. So we should start our life with yoga as it is not only important for our body but also relaxes our soul. After getting energy from the universe we can control our breath. Yoga is not a religion; it is a practice and is beneficial for everyone on earth. Yoga connects our body, mind, and soul. If we are physically fit, only then we will be able to connect with the divine powers of the universe. By practicing yoga, not only our body but our mind and views will also be pure.

Benefits of Yoga:

It helps relax our mind

Improves our flexibility

Controls our blood pressure

Builds muscle strength

Boosts our immunity

Helps in healing

Perfects our posture

Improves our breathing system

Improves our mood

Reduces stress level

There are four types of yoga; while there are many more types, you should know the four major forms:

Bhakti Yoga

Karma Yoga

Gyan Yoga

Raj Yoga

Bhakti yoga means to serve God in this form of yoga. The Yogi gets deep knowledge of God, and God accepts those who are truly devoted to Him.

Karma Yoga – Nobody is away from karmas because everybody has to work; if no one will do karmas, the *shristhi* will stop.

Gyan Yoga means that we should read good spiritual books to gain knowledge and be on the right path.

Raj Yoga means we have to meet our inner soul and we will be able to take good decisions.

My Teachers' Blessings

Hello,

Namaste.

I am Swati .P. Midha. I am a Reiki healer. This is a field where the more you learn the more you have an opportunity to explore and learn further. Sunita Verma is a very dear friend, more like a sister. While I have been on the spiritual path for the last 15 years, her journey started 5 years ago, and her growth has been immense. Her journey started when she was facing some issue in her life which is very common and normal. I introduced her to the art of living by Sri Sri Ravi Shankar, who is my guru, and I also tell my family he is my *Bade Papa*.

One day, Sunita called me to give her healing, and I encouraged her to learn to heal herself rather than asking me. This was her call into the world of spirituality. She started her initial course from me, followed by two more courses, and then there has been no looking back for her. She pursed many more courses from other teachers as well, and today I am immensely proud of her journey. She is a devotee of Maa, and Maa loves her a lot. She is a wonderful healer; her healing is powerful, amazing, and magical.

This is so sweet of her to give me the honor to write for her book, and I am blessed that she chose me to be her first teacher for the magic of universe.

Today, Sunita is not only an excellent healer but also a very good friend of mine. I wish her loads of love and luck, and I also pray for her to be happy and successful in all spheres of life as she has been chosen by God to make this world a better place.

Love you, dear Sunita.

Namaskar,

I am Vikas Duggal. I want to talk you through this writing. Friends, Adhyatmic Vikas Mission (AVM) was established through Sai Baba, and we are running it with his grace. Sai Baba connects the people with the institute if he wants them connected with us. ADM is where it is today because of his blessings. In this institute, we teach a lot of courses like Reiki Healing, Angel Therapy, Crystal Healing, and many more. One day we met Sunita Verma as she came to our institute and learned a lot of courses from us and learned all of them with her full heart. Meeting her was a good experience. She is such an angelic personality who always thinks good for others, and she has dedicated and devoted herself for people who need her as she will clear all her karmic account.

We wish that God gives her a chance to become an angel in the next birth as well. I feel that I have met Sunita and taught her the way you teach a pure soul, which has been a very good experience. We feel proud as we come to know of her healing results and dhayan experiences. We always wish for all our students to be like her, and we are lucky to have such a student in our institute. We wish that blessings of Sai Baba may always be with her and angels guide her on her path. Sunita is writing a book and we wish her good luck. This book will go a long way as she is writing it with sacred feelings.

Again wishing good luck and encouraging more people on the path of spirituality.

Sanjay Gupta, a teacher of Lama Fera:

Om Sai Ram

I wish divine soul Sunita Verma ji the very best in her spiritual journey and look forward to her autobiography. She is an angel, queen of healing, connected with the higher universal energies with deep knowledge of various healing modalities. She works endlessly to remove the bad effects of karma through her holistic healing to create, trust, grow, and glow manifest and healing.

Sanjay Gupta

My Journey to Spirituality

This is my first book, and I have written this book with energies from the universe and blessings of Maa. Herein I have written my own experiences in a simple language, and this is a very pure book for me. My purpose of writing this book is to bring more and more people toward spirituality. I am a very simple person; if I can go on the path of spirituality, then anyone can. All of us have problems in life. We should not run from them or go here and there or even ask other people to solve them, but we should ourselves move toward spirituality, sit for meditation, and pray to God to help us solve these problems. If we do so, our problems will be solved automatically.

I hope you all will like my book, so I can get encouraged to write the next book.